D1260117

Searchlight
BOOKS™

Do You
Know the
Continents?

Learning about North America

Christine Petersen

Lerner Publications ◆ Minneapolis

Content Consultant: Ryan Weichelt, PhD, Assistant Professor of Geography and
Anthropology, University of Wisconsin Eau-Claire

Lerner Publications Company
A division of Lerner Publishing Group, Inc.
241 First Avenue North
Minneapolis, MN 55401 USA

For reading levels and more information, look up this title at www.lernerbooks.com.

Library of Congress Cataloging-in-Publication Data

Petersen, Christine.
        Learning about North America / by Christine Petersen.
            pages cm. — (Searchlight books. Do you know the continents?)
        Includes index.
        Audience: Grades 4 to 6.
        ISBN 978-1-4677-8020-9 (lb : alk. paper) — ISBN 978-1-4677-8353-8
    (pb : alk. paper) — ISBN 978-1-4677-8354-5 (eb pdf)
        1. North America—Juvenile literature. I. Title.
    E38.5.P47 2015
    970—dc23   2015000305

Manufactured in the United States of America
1 – VP – 7/15/15

Contents

Chapter 1

A DIVERSE LAND

North America is the third largest of the seven continents. It spans half the globe. It touches the ice caps of the North Pole and stretches to the tropical rain forests near the equator.

North America is a big place. Which pole is North America closest to?

NORTH AMERICA COVERS MORE THAN 9 MILLION SQUARE MILES (24 MILLION SQUARE KILOMETERS).

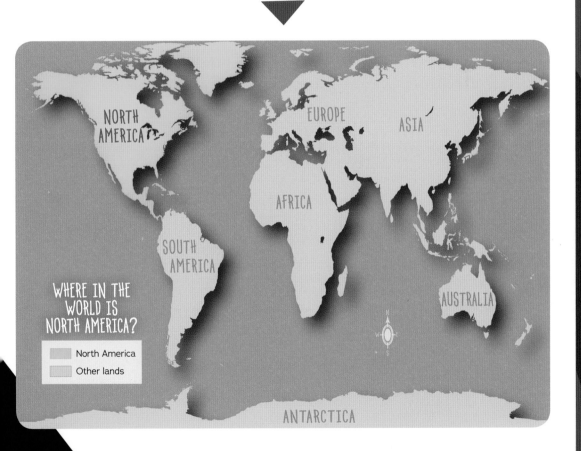

NORTH AMERICA

EUROPE

ASIA

AFRICA

SOUTH AMERICA

AUSTRALIA

WHERE IN THE WORLD IS NORTH AMERICA?

North America
Other lands

ANTARCTICA

Large and Small Countries

Canada and the United States are the two largest countries in North America. South of the United States is Mexico. The seven nations of Central America are farther south. Central America is not its own continent. It is part of North America. The countries in Central America connect North America to South America. Thirteen island nations are also among North America's many countries. These tiny nations are in the Caribbean Sea. They are part of a group of more than seven thousand islands.

Caribbean island nations are famous for their warm waters.

THE PANAMA CANAL CUTS ACROSS
PANAMA IN CENTRAL AMERICA TO CONNECT
THE ATLANTIC AND PACIFIC OCEANS.

Giant sequoias rise high in the western United States.

Large and Diverse

North America features many diverse cultures and climates. It has everything from hills and mountains to forests and plains. Small lakes dot parts of North America. Vast oceans lie along its coasts. There is something for everyone in North America!

Greenland

Greenland is the world's largest island. It is in the North Atlantic Ocean. It is a part of the European country of Denmark—yet Greenland is still considered part of North America. That's because of where it is located. Greenland is just east of northern Canada. Greenland is approximately fifty times as large as the rest of Denmark. But one hundred times as many people live in Denmark! That's because Greenland is so icy and cold.

Chapter 2

COUNTRIES AND CITIES

Canada is in the far north of North America. The First Nations and the Inuit people lived in Canada for thousands of years before anyone else came to the land. French and British fur traders reached Canada in the 1500s. Great Britain and France ruled Canada for nearly 250 years. Canada became its own country in 1867.

People have lived in Canada for thousands of years. What were Canada's first people called?

Canada is the second-largest country in the world. Only Russia is bigger. But the United States has ten times more people. More than thirty million people live in Canada. More than three hundred million live in the United States.

Most Canadians live in big cities in the south, such as Toronto.

Christopher Columbus's arrival in the Caribbean led the way for other Europeans to cross the Atlantic Ocean to North America.

The United States

The United States is south of Canada. Millions of American Indians lived in what is now the United States before Europeans arrived. The Europeans claimed the land as their own. They took it by force. European immigrants formed the United States of America in 1776.

The descendants of both the European immigrants and the American Indians live in the country now. The nation is also home to many other peoples. They trace their roots to Africa, Asia, South America, and more. They live in cities, suburbs, and rural areas. Some of the biggest cities in the United States are New York, Los Angeles, and Chicago.

Chicago is the third-biggest city in the United States.

Mexico

South of the United States is Mexico. Spanish explorers invaded the land starting in 1519. The explorers met indigenous peoples, including the Aztecs. The Spanish conquered the Aztecs and other peoples.

Ruins of ancient cities can still be found in Mexico.

Spain controlled Mexico for the next three hundred years. Spain also ruled the modern countries of Central America and even parts of the United States.

LOCATE MEXICO ON THE MAP. WHAT COUNTRIES DOES IT BORDER?

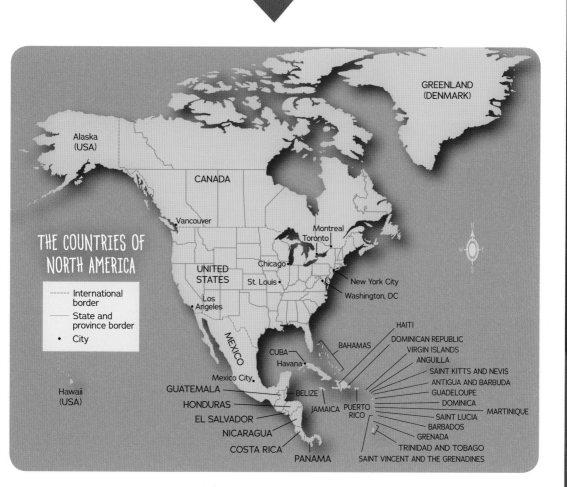

THE COUNTRIES OF NORTH AMERICA

GREENLAND (DENMARK)

Alaska (USA)

CANADA

Vancouver

Montreal
Toronto

Chicago

UNITED STATES   St. Louis

Los Angeles

New York City
Washington, DC

- - - - - International border
——— State and province border
• City

HAITI

HAWAII (USA)

Hawaii (USA)

MEXICO

CUBA
Havana

BAHAMAS

DOMINICAN REPUBLIC
VIRGIN ISLANDS
ANGUILLA
SAINT KITTS AND NEVIS
ANTIGUA AND BARBUDA
GUADELOUPE
DOMINICA
MARTINIQUE
SAINT LUCIA
BARBADOS
GRENADA
TRINIDAD AND TOBAGO

Mexico City

GUATEMALA
HONDURAS
EL SALVADOR
NICARAGUA
COSTA RICA
PANAMA

BELIZE

JAMAICA PUERTO RICO

SAINT VINCENT AND THE GRENADINES

El Salvador is the smallest country in Central America.

Caribbean and Central American Nations

The seven countries in Central America are much smaller than Canada, the United States, and Mexico. Guatemala lies south of Mexico. Almost half of Guatemalans are descended from Maya. The Maya ruled much of Central America and southern Mexico. Guatemala and other Central American countries won independence from Spain in the 1800s.

Cuba is the largest Caribbean country. Approximately eleven million people live there. Indigenous peoples lived in the Caribbean countries before Europeans came. Many Caribbean countries, including Jamaica, lost and later regained independence. The Arawak people lived in what is now Jamaica before Europeans came. Spain took over Jamaica in the late 1400s. England invaded and took over in 1655. Jamaica finally became a country in 1962.

Jamaica is full of natural wonders such as this waterfall.

Chichén Itzá

The Maya were a very large group of indigenous peoples. They lived in southern Mexico and Central America. Chichén Itzá was one big Maya city. A huge pyramid is in the center of Chichén Itzá. It honors the Maya god Kukulkan. More than six million Maya still live in Mexico and Central America.

Chapter 3

LANDFORMS AND CLIMATE

North America is a land of extremes. Can you climb its highest mountain? Alaska's Mount McKinley stands 20,320 feet (6,194 meters) tall. Or you could try walking in Death Valley. It is the lowest spot in North America. It is also the hottest place on Earth. It was 134°F (57°C) on July 10, 1913!

North America has hot and cold places. Where in North America is the hottest place on Earth?

Land of Waters

North America has water on three sides. The Atlantic Ocean meets the East Coast. The Pacific Ocean is to the west. Far to the north is the Arctic Ocean. Parts of it are frozen all year. The Gulf of Mexico is a huge bay. It is nearly as large as Alaska. Canada's Hudson Bay is another huge body of water. North America also has many big lakes and rivers. The Great Lakes between Canada and the United States are famous around the world.

The Mississippi River is the fourth-longest river in the world.

Parícutin is a volcano in the Transvolcanic Mountains. It erupted for the first time in 1943.

Soaring Mountain Chains

The Rocky Mountains soar in the western United States and Canada. The Appalachian Mountains are a long chain in the eastern United States. Mexico's Transvolcanic Mountains run across the country's southern region.

Climate

North America has a wide variety of climates. The areas in the north are cold tundra climates. There is little rain and snow. Not many people live there. Southern Canada and much of the United States have mild climates. They have four seasons. These areas are great for growing crops.

The southwestern United States and much of Mexico are covered in semiarid and desert areas. They are dry without much rain. And Central America and the Caribbean nations have tropical climates. These are warm places. They get a lot of rain.

Compare the satellite image of North America to the physical map on the right. How do different climates change what the land looks like from space?

WHICH CLIMATE ZONES HAVE YOU LIVED IN OR VISITED?

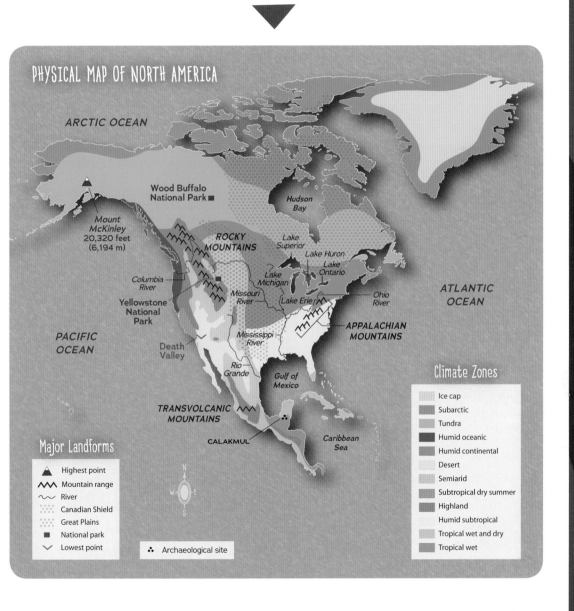

PHYSICAL MAP OF NORTH AMERICA

ARCTIC OCEAN

Wood Buffalo
National Park ■

Hudson
Bay

Mount
McKinley
20,320 feet
(6,194 m)

ROCKY
MOUNTAINS

Lake
Superior

Lake Huron

Lake
Ontario

Columbia
River

Lake
Michigan

Missouri
River

Lake Erie

Ohio
River

ATLANTIC
OCEAN

Yellowstone
National
Park

APPALACHIAN
MOUNTAINS

PACIFIC
OCEAN

Death
Valley

Mississippi
River

Rio
Grande

Gulf of
Mexico

TRANSVOLCANIC
MOUNTAINS

CALAKMUL

Caribbean
Sea

Climate Zones

- Ice cap
- Subarctic
- Tundra
- Humid oceanic
- Humid continental
- Desert
- Semiarid
- Subtropical dry summer
- Highland
- Humid subtropical
- Tropical wet and dry
- Tropical wet

Major Landforms

- ▲ Highest point
- ᴧᴧᴧ Mountain range
- ∿ River
- Canadian Shield
- Great Plains
- ■ National park
- ⋁ Lowest point

N
W E
S

⁂ Archaeological site

Chapter 4

NATURAL RESOURCES

North America's natural resources include a wide variety of plants and animals. These resources are different depending on which area of the continent you are in. Plants grow low to the ground on the tundra in the north. But these short plants feed huge herds of caribou. The northern oceans are full of schools of fish. Whales and walrus live there.

There is life in the far north. What kinds of animals feed on tundra plants?

The Great Plains and Southern Warmth

Huge plains fill the heart of North America. Grasslands once covered this region. They stretched as far as the eye could see. The Great Plains were home to bison and wolves. The Great Plains were cleared for crops. Farmers have replaced tall prairie grasses with corn and wheat.

Northern Mexico is covered in desert. Cacti and shrubs grow here. They require little water to survive. Birds called roadrunners dash across the desert floor. Prairie dogs dig into the dry ground.

Farther south into Central America there is more rain. Monkeys swing between the rain forest trees. Long-nosed anteaters sniff out insects. Colorful fish swim in coral reefs. Would you like to go for a swim? The Caribbean is full of sandy beaches.

Toucans and other colorful birds make their homes in Central America.

National Parks

National parks are some of North America's most beautiful natural resources. Yellowstone National Park in Wyoming became the world's first national park in 1872. It is famous for its geysers and hot springs. Old Faithful (BELOW) is one of the best-known geysers in the world. Wood Buffalo National Park in Canada protects the rare wood bison that live in the mountains.

Chapter 5

PEOPLE AND CULTURES

More than five hundred million people live in North America. They represent a wide variety of backgrounds and age groups. The average age of Americans and Canadians is rising. Mexico is a younger country. Approximately one-third of Mexicans are under the age of fifteen. The country's population

North America has several large countries. Which has the youngest population?

First Peoples

Before about fifty thousand years ago, there were no people in North America at all. Around that time, the first people arrived on the continent. They came from Asia by boat or across a land bridge. The bridge connected Russia to Alaska. They were the ancestors of modern American Indian peoples. In the 1500s, European people began arriving in North America in large numbers.

Some American Indian peoples built cities into the sides of cliffs in the desert.

Jazz music blends many different musical styles.

US Melting Pot

People from around the world have been coming to the United States ever since. The country is often described as a melting pot of cultures. These cultures have changed the United States. Jazz was created in the South in the early 1900s. It combines African and European musical styles. Others brought bits of their cultures too. Latin Americans brought traditional foods such as tacos, for example. And Asian immigrants introduced K-pop. This high-energy style of music has been popular in Asia for years.

Spanish Heritage

More than 140 million people live in Mexico and Central America. Spanish is the official language in Mexico and all Central American countries except Belize.

Mexican and Central American people are mostly descendants of Spanish invaders and the indigenous people. Most Mexicans and Central Americans follow the Roman Catholic religion.

North America has people that come from nearly every religious and cultural background in the world. Arabs, Jews, and American Indians all have a vital place in North American life. Immigrants have come to North America from just about every country on Earth.

New York City is one of North America's most diverse cities.

Ojibwe Powwows

American Indian cultures have been passed down through the generations in North America. The Ojibwe American Indians traditionally lived in the north central United States and south central Canada. One of the most important Ojibwe traditions is the powwow. People from all around gather to sing, dance, and honor their ancestors. A modern powwow may last as long as four days.

Chapter 6

ECONOMICS

Many people in North America make a living from the continent's rich energy and mineral resources. Oil, gas, and coal fuel vehicles and provide electricity. Zinc, lead, and nickel come from North American mines. These metals are used in computers and cell phones. Both Mexico and the United States make money from useful metals such as iron and steel. California was famous for its gold in the mid-1800s.

North America has many mineral resources. What are oil, coal, and gas used for?

Forests and Farms

Other North Americans make a living by logging and farming. Loggers get lumber from the pine forests of the United States and Canada. They often plant new trees to make sure future generations have lumber too.

Lumber is big business in North America.

Fruit and vegetable growers are spread across the continent. The Central Valley of California, the Rio Grande Valley in Texas, and the highland areas of Mexico produce strawberries, tomatoes, and avocados. Farmers from the Great Plains ship grain worldwide. The American South ships out cotton. If you like bananas or sugar, thank the Caribbean nations. Your mom or dad might buy coffee grown in Central America.

Coffee beans from Central America get shipped all around the world.

WHICH NATURAL RESOURCES ARE FOUND NEAR WHERE YOU LIVE?

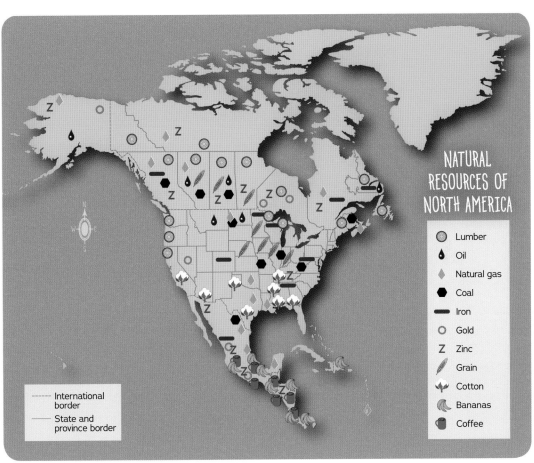

NATURAL RESOURCES OF NORTH AMERICA

- ◎ Lumber
- ◗ Oil
- ◆ Natural gas
- ⬡ Coal
- ▬ Iron
- ○ Gold
- Z Zinc
- 🌾 Grain
- 🌱 Cotton
- 🍌 Bananas
- ☕ Coffee

------- International border

——— State and province border

A Changed Land

North America has vast natural resources, but getting these resources can sometimes harm the land. The European settlers changed the continent in many ways. They cut down forests and dug into mountains. Governments later began protecting North America's amazing landscapes.

Adventures in North America

People come from around the world to explore North American cities and scenery. They admire the continent's natural wonders and cultural icons.

Devils Tower in Wyoming is just one natural wonder North America has to offer.

Exploring North America

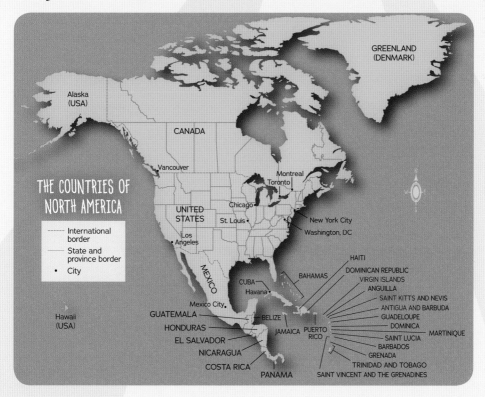

The Countries of North America map, showing:

GREENLAND (DENMARK)

Alaska (USA)

CANADA

Vancouver

Montreal
Toronto

THE COUNTRIES OF NORTH AMERICA

Legend:
- ------ International border
- ——— State and province border
- • City

UNITED STATES

Chicago
St. Louis
Los Angeles
New York City
Washington, DC

Hawaii (USA)

MEXICO

Mexico City

CUBA
Havana

HAITI
DOMINICAN REPUBLIC
VIRGIN ISLANDS
ANGUILLA
SAINT KITTS AND NEVIS
ANTIGUA AND BARBUDA
GUADELOUPE
DOMINICA
MARTINIQUE
SAINT LUCIA
BARBADOS
GRENADA

BAHAMAS

GUATEMALA
HONDURAS
EL SALVADOR
NICARAGUA
COSTA RICA

BELIZE
JAMAICA
PUERTO RICO

PANAMA

TRINIDAD AND TOBAGO
SAINT VINCENT AND THE GRENADINES

Choose two or three countries or cities from the map above that you want to know more about. Choose places from different parts of North America. Research these places online. What unique things are there to see and do? What do people eat? What local celebrations or festivals take place there? Write a paragraph about a trip you will take to each place. What will you see and do?

Glossary

ancestor: a relative who lived long ago

climate: a place's weather over a long period of time

descendant: someone related to a person or people who lived a long time ago

equator: an imaginary line around the center of the world

geyser: a hole in the ground that erupts with water or steam

immigrant: a person who moves to a country where he or she was not born. Many people have immigrated to North America from other countries.

plains: wide, flat areas of land. The central United States is covered by the Great Plains.

prairie: a type of land covered in tall grasses. Much of central North America used to be prairie.

tundra: in arctic regions, a huge, mostly flat area where no trees grow

LERNER

SOURCE

Expand learning beyond the printed book. Download free, complementary educational resources for this book from our website, www.lerneresource.com.

Learn More about North America

Books

Gimpel, Diane Marczely. *A Timeline History of Early American Indian Peoples*. Minneapolis: Lerner Publications, 2015. Learn about the American Indians who lived in North America before the Europeans arrived there.

Harrison, David L. *Mammoth Bones and Broken Stones: The Mystery of North America's First People*. Honesdale, PA: Boyds Mills Press, 2010. Learn about how archaeologists find out what life was like in ancient North America.

Woods, Mary B., and Michael Woods. *Seven Wonders of Ancient North America*. Minneapolis: Twenty-First Century Books, 2009. Learn about the pyramids, the temples, and other wonders that the ancient people of North America built.

Websites

Central America and the Caribbean Geography
http://www.ducksters.com/geography/centralamerica.php
Find out about the geography and the environment of the countries and the islands in the Caribbean Sea.

***National Geographic* Atlas Puzzles**
http://ngm.nationalgeographic.com/map/atlas/puzzles
Test your knowledge of North American geography by putting together a jigsaw puzzle of the continent.

***National Geographic:* Mexico**
http://kids.nationalgeographic.com/explore/countries/mexico
Read this website to learn more about Mexico, the country that borders the United States to the south.

Index

Photo Acknowledgments

The images in this book are used with the permission of: © Marc Parsons/Shutterstock Images, p. 4; © Laura Westlund/Independent Picture Service, pp. 5, 15, 23, 35, 37; © SeanPavonePhoto/ iStock/Thinkstock, p. 6; © onlymehdi/iStockphoto, p. 7; © welcomia/Shutterstock Images, p. 8; © Koonyongyut/iStock/Thinkstock, p. 9; © Danita Delimont/Alamy, p. 10; © SurangaSL/ Shutterstock Images, p. 11; Library of Congress, p. 12 (LC-DIG-pga-02388); © MaxyM/Shutterstock Images, p. 13; © Hugo Brizard/Shutterstock Images, p. 14; © Stefano Ember/Shutterstock Images, p. 16; © Jason Cowell/iStockphoto, p. 17; © jgorzynik/Shutterstock Images, p. 18; © David Persson/ Shutterstock Images, p. 19; © Nancy Bauer/Shutterstock Images, p. 20; © InterFoto/Alamy, p. 21; © Anton Balazh/Shutterstock Images, p. 22; © Richard Seeley/iStockphoto, p. 24; © Eduardo Rivero/Shutterstock Images, p. 25; © Lorcel/Shutterstock Images, p. 26; © Eye Ubiquitous/ Newscom, p. 27; © Nick Harris/Virgil Pomfret Agency/Thinkstock, p. 28; © Jose Gil/Shutterstock Images, p. 29; © Jay Lazarin/iStockphoto, p. 30; © Tony Bock/ZumaPress/Newscom, p. 31; © wlfella/iStock/Thinkstock, p. 32; © abadonian/iStock/Thinkstock, p. 33; © haak78/Shutterstock Images, p. 34; © Richard A. McMillin/Shutterstock Images, p. 36.

Cover image: © Planet Observer/Universal Images via Getty Images.

Main body text set in Adrianna Regular 14/20.
Typeface provided by Chank.